Quick, Easy, Keto

5-Minute Ketogenic Diet
Recipes for Beginners

Table of Contents

Keto - Quick and Easy

"Give me a one-page bullet-list of exactly what I should do. That's worth more to me than a stack of books that I have to dig through to get to the good stuff. I may give you 50 bucks for the books. But I'll pay you $5,000 for the one page."

-Alwyn Cosgrove, world famous strength coach

Thank you for buying this book.

While there are a LOT of great resources online for beginners new to the ketogenic diet, we wanted to boil it down and give you the meat and potatoes (*well, scratch the potatoes... but you know what I mean*)

The premise of this book is to give quick and easy ketogenic meals that you can make in 5-minutes.

It's a tall order, we know.

But we worked really hard to give you simple to make, delicious, healthy ketogenic recipes.

Enjoy!

[**Disclaimer**: Please follow the advice of your doctor before starting any diet or exercise program. The information in this book is for informational purposes and is not meant to treat diseases or promise miracle results.. Do not forgo, dismiss, or ignore advice from trained medical professions - especially if you have a health condition.

That said, we hope you enjoy this book!]

Keto For Beginners: What Makes The Ketogenic Diet Different?

There are TONS of diets out there.

Enough to make you crazy.

Here's a quick summary of the most popular ones and how they compare to keto.

Atkins Diet – Though both diets are low in carbohydrates, the keto diet focuses on fat consumption and there are recommended ratios for carbohydrates, protein, and fats. The Atkins diet is more concerned with its four phases, with one leading to short term ketosis. The maintenance phase of the Atkins diet is decidedly not as low carb as you would be on the keto diet.

Paleo Diet – The Paleo diet is grain-free, gluten-free, and dairy-free with an emphasis on fresh fruits, vegetables, nuts, and lean protein. The ketogenic diet focuses more on fatty proteins like red meat as well as dairy products like heavy cream. Both diets are designed for long-term use and provide many health benefits.

Mediterranean Diet – The Mediterranean diet places heavy emphasis on healthy fats (particularly omega-3 fatty acids) but also includes a lot of whole grains and high-carb veggies. Both are intended for long-term use and can support weight loss as well as numerous health benefits.

Gluten-Free Diet – A medical necessity for people with gluten allergies and celiac disease, the gluten-free diet is also a popular health trend. This type of diet is free from gluten-containing grains but there are no other restrictions. There is some overlap between the gluten-free and ketogenic diets because many gluten-free alternatives like almond flour and coconut flour fit well into the low-carb, high-fat keto diet.

Clean Eating – Not a specific diet but a dietary choice, clean eating involves eating only whole, minimally processed foods. This type of diet tends to be high in whole grains, fruits, and veggies which is a departure from the fat-centric ketogenic diet, though both include plenty of protein from healthy sources.

Detoxes and Cleanses – Whether it's juicing, smoothies, or fasting, detox diets and cleanses are usually very low in calories and fat. These diets are designed to cleanse the body of accumulated toxins and to encourage rapid weight loss but most of it ends up being water weight. The ketogenic diet is a long-term choice and doesn't put as much stress on the system as crash diets.

Vegan and Vegetarian – These diets limit or exclude animal products such as meat and eggs – the focus is on excluding these foods rather than restricting calories. The ketogenic diet is different because there is a heavy emphasis on animal products like bacon, eggs, and red meat as well as dairy products (which are excluded from the vegan diet).

By now you should have a better understanding of what the ketogenic diet is and how it is different from other diets.

In the next chapter, we'll take a closer look at the benefits of the ketogenic diet. You'll also receive helpful information for fasting while on the ketogenic diet and some precautions to take before starting the diet.

Why Keto? Benefits Of The Keto Diet

While not universally accepted, there are quite a few benefits to the keto diet. Below is a quick summary.

Epilepsy: Keto has long known to benefit epileptic patients. Research conducted back in 1921 showed that switching to a Ketogenic diet has resulted in a lowered incidence of seizures. Exercise care and professional supervision - and under no circumstances should you dismiss medical advice.

Reversing the Effects of Type 2 Diabetes: Another reported benefit is that in some cases, the keto diet can reverse the effects of type 2 diabetes. It makes sense that lowering carbs would help, but **don't** forgo medical advice from a trained professional. A severe drop in blood sugar can cause dizziness and fatigue (but you already know that).

Weight Loss: As your body shifts from burning carbs as fuel to burning fat, many people report increased weight loss. It's not magic though, often times it's because cutting out carbs causes people to eat less.

Better Focus: Lots of people report increased focus after fully switching to keto. It's hard to get into keto (old habits die hard!) but once you're in keto, almost everyone swears by its cognitive effects.

Acne Reduction: Lots of people experience improvements in their acne. Some say acne is mostly caused and driven by insulin. So cutting out carbs, and lowering protein intake reduces the flood of insulin the body produces that may lead to acne.

Slower the Effects Aging: Ketogenic diet, your body can and will look younger for longer. Not to get all scientific on you, but when you enter ketosis, your body may block a group of enzymes known as histone deacetylases. The enzymes function to keep a couple of genes known as Forkhead box O3 and Metallothionein 2A turned off. These genes can empower other cells to resist oxidative stress. The good thing is that the ketones produced during full fledged ketosis can block Forkhead box O3 allowing the genes to be reactivated which prevents oxidative stress because it is this oxidative stress that indirectly causes aging.

Alzheimer's Disease: In addition to helping prevent epileptic seizures, keto has been reported to prevent Alzheimer's disease.

Prepping for Keto

While the specific benefits of the Keto diet are not as compelling as many people expect, you may still want to try it yourself, especially under a stricter approach. This is where it is important to note that there are some small preparation steps you can take when looking to maximize your success with the diet.

Preparing for the foods you are about to consume is key. The planning stage can make or break the diet and this is why you need to prepare in advance. The first thing you need to anticipate is the elimination of the carbohydrates from your diet.

Consider Lowering Carbohydrates (duh!)

Adapting to keto is brutal in the first few weeks, so you should experiment with the low-carbohydrate approach for an entire day before deciding to go on the diet. The Ketogenic diet is very strict when it comes to the foods you can consume and to those which you exclude. Since you are going to exclude all grains and their nutrients, you can even begin to do this on certain days before the diet, not because of the weight loss benefits but to better establish the types of foods you can source and the types of meals you can prepare.

It's easy to find keto foods (meat, oil, butter, cheese, nuts, avocado, greens, etc.) you also need to consider their overall

cost and quality as well. But most importantly, you need to
see if they are actually sustainable for your daily meals with
your own lifestyle. Some things to consider include:

The Time Needed To Prepare Meals

Some meals take longer to prepare than others. If you have a
busy schedule and especially if you have a family to look
after, realize that you will need to prepare separate meals for
yourself. This involves more time in the kitchen and in many
cases, preparing the meals in advance can be the only option
if you want to save time.

Meals You Can Consume At Work

While away from home, you can find that sticking to the diet
can be more challenging. This is where you might be tempted
by various quick snacks which are often very high in
carbohydrates. The best solution is to prepare your meals in
advance and take them with you to work. If this is not
possible, you should always have a Keto supplement on hand
to provide your body the nutrition it needs during this
otherwise stressful period.

Resting Time

You need to get enough sleep every night, especially during
the first and the second week of the diet when your body
begins to adapt to the dietary changes. In some cases, people

are fine with only 6 hours of sleep every night but since you might feel more tired while on the Keto diet, you might need to get at least 8 hours of sleep every night. To make this achievable, you will need to go to bed early or even switch off electronics such as the TV or phone before going to bed in order to fall asleep faster.

Workouts and Physical Activity

If you plan to stay active on the diet, you can expect a drop in performance which can come in various forms. It is here that you can expect to lift lighter weights if you train at the gym. But you can also expect lower endurance if you are a fan of cardio. You need to plan your training accordingly with shorter workouts. At the same time, you can consider the supplements which are made specifically for this goal and the active people on the Keto diet.

Set a Budget and Start Saving

Setting a budget for the Keto diet is highly recommended. The foods you consume within 30 days are not cheap and you may even want to add some supplements to achieve the best results. Calculating a daily budget for foods is a good idea.

The price should not be the only variable to consider when it comes to making better choices. Food quality is also important. Fresh produce is crucial and you can do all you can to get these types of foods. A good idea is to look at the foods you can source from your local farmers market. In many cases, you can find great foods like meats and eggs which are even healthier than the options you find in supermarkets. At the same time, you also have the ability to find fresh seasonal foods at a farmers market. Therefore, instead of consuming frozen foods with not much nutritional value, you can focus on fresh ingredients which are always recommended for weight loss.

Buy In Bulk

Bulk buying is one of the best tips you can apply when preparing for the Keto diet. Many foods can be cheaper this way and you can start with the basics and make your way up to the least essential foods. This is where it is worth considering the options you have at your local supermarkets. Many of these shops have new offers every week so it is worth seeing what is on sale on your particular dieting week.

Plan Fat Intake

Fats represent the most important macronutrient on the Ketogenic diet. With 75% of the total daily nutritional intake, fats need to be planned before you actually start the diet. At the very least, you should know where to buy the fats you need when you begin the diet. Saturated fats, monosaturated fats and polyunsaturated fats such as Omega 3 are recommended on the Keto diet.

Chapter 3:

Breakfast Recipes

Wholesome Breakfast Eggs

Prep Time: 5 min.
Cooking Time: 5 min.
Number of Servings: 2-3

Ingredients:

- ¼ teaspoon cumin, ground
- 4 eggs
- ½ teaspoon sea salt
- ¼ teaspoon ground cayenne
- 1 teaspoon thyme leaves
- 2 garlic cloves, peeled and chopped finely
- ½ cup parsley, chopped
- ½ cup cilantro, chopped
- 2 tablespoons butter
- 1 tablespoon coconut oil

Directions:

1. Arrange your Instant Pot over a dry, clean platform. Plug it in power socket and turn it on.
2. Now press "Saute" mode from available options. In the cooking area, add the butter, oil, and garlic; cook for 1-2 minutes to soften the added ingredients.
3. Add thyme and cook for a minute. Mix in the parsley and cilantro and cook until it starts to crisp for around 2 minutes.
4. Take the eggs and break into the pan; do not to break the yolks.

5. Close the lid and lock. Ensure that you have sealed the valve to avoid leakage.
6. Keep the pot on sauté function and cook for 2 minutes.
7. Open the lid and serve warm!

Nutritional Values (Per Serving):

Calories – 310

Fat – 27g

Carbohydrates – 3g

Fiber – 1g

Protein – 12.5g

Wholesome Turkey Bacon Muffins

Prep Time: 5 min.
Cooking Time: 5 min.
Number of Servings: 5

Ingredients:
- 1 green onion, diced
- 1/4 tsp. lemon pepper seasoning
- 4 medium eggs
- 4 tablespoons cheddar cheese, shredded
- 4 slices turkey bacon (precooked), crumbled

Directions:
1. In a bowl of medium size, whisk the eggs; mix in the pepper and mix well.
2. Divide the green onion, bacon, and cheese into the muffin cups. Top with the egg mixture and stir gently.
3. Arrange your Instant Pot over a dry, clean platform. Plug it in power socket and turn it on.
4. Pour the water (1 ½ cups) in the pot. Arrange the trivet inside and add the cups over the trivet.
5. Close the lid and lock. Ensure that you have sealed the valve to avoid leakage.
6. Press "Manual" mode from available cooking settings and set cooking time to 8 minutes. Instant Pot will start cooking the ingredients after a few minutes.

7. After the timer reads zero, press "Cancel"; press "NPR" to naturally release pressure. It takes about 5 minutes to release pressure naturally.
8. Carefully remove the lid and serve the prepared keto dish warm!

Nutritional Values (Per Serving):

Calories – 132

Fat – 10.5g

Carbohydrates – 1g

Fiber – 0g

Protein – 9.5g

Avocado Egg Morning

Prep Time: 5 min.
Cooking Time: 5 min.
Number of Servings: 4

Ingredients:

- 2 tablespoons green onions, finely chopped
- 1 teaspoon olive oil
- 1 medium-sized avocado, pitted and cubed
- 2 large eggs, beaten
- 1 tablespoon butter
- ½ teaspoon sea salt
- ¼ teaspoon red chili flakes
- ¼ teaspoon (ground) black pepper
- Milk (optional)

Directions:

1. Take your Instant Pot; open the top lid. Plug it and turn it on.
2. Press "SAUTÉ" setting and the pot will start heating up.
3. In the cooking pot area, add the butter and avocado cubes. Season with pepper and salt.
4. Cook until starts becoming softened for 2-3 minutes. Stir in between.
5. Add the eggs, green onions, and olive oil. Optionally, add 2 tablespoons of milk for a creamier texture.
6. Stir and cook for 3 minutes, or until the eggs are set.

7. Press "Cancel". Add in serving bowls and enjoy.

Nutritional Values (Per Serving):
Calories – 321
Fat – 32g
Carbohydrates – 12g
Fiber – 7g
Protein – 8.5g

Baked Turkey Bacon Egg

Prep Time: 5 min.
Cooking Time: 5 min.
Number of Servings: 4

Ingredients:
- 8 eggs
- ½ cup milk
- 1 cup mozzarella cheese, shredded
- ¼ cup green onions, chopped
- ½ teaspoon salt
- 8 pieces bacon, chopped
- 2 cups cauliflower, chopped

Directions:
1. Take your Instant Pot; open the top lid. Plug it and turn it on.
2. Press "SAUTÉ" setting and the pot will start heating up.
3. In the cooking pot area, add the oil and bacon. Stir and cook until evenly brown from all sides.
4. Using a wooden spatula spread the bacon evenly over the bottom.
5. Add the cauliflower on top.
6. In another bowl, whisk the eggs and season with salt. Pour in the milk and whisk together until turn foamy.
7. Add the mixture over cauliflower and top with mozzarella cheese.

8. Close the top lid and seal its valve.
9. Press "MANUAL" setting. Adjust cooking time to 5 minutes.
10. Allow the recipe to cook for the set cooking time.
11. After the set cooking time ends, press "CANCEL" and then press "QPR (Quick Pressure Release)".
12. Instant Pot will quickly release the pressure.
13. Open the top lid, add the cooked recipe mix in serving plates.
14. Sprinkle with green onions and serve immediately.

Nutritional Values (Per Serving):

Calories - 298

Fat – 26g

Carbohydrates – 8g

Fiber – 1.5g

Protein – 29g

Turkey Sausage Egg Pie

Prep Time: 5 min.
Cooking Time: 5 min.
Number of Servings: 7-8

Ingredients:
- ½ cup diced onion
- 3 teaspoons olive oil
- ¼ cup grated parmesan cheese
- 1 pound turkey sausage
- 2 cups ricotta cheese
- 1 garlic clove, minced
- 1 cup shredded mozzarella cheese
- 3 eggs
- Pepper and salt, as needed
- 8 cups chopped Swiss chard
- 2 cups water

Directions:
1. Take your Instant Pot; open the top lid. Plug it and turn it on.
2. Press "SAUTÉ" setting and the pot will start heating up.
3. In the cooking pot area, add the oil, garlic, and onions. Cook until starts becoming translucent and softened for 3 minutes. Stir in between.
4. Add chard and cook for 2 minutes, or until it becomes wilted.

5. Season with some pepper and salt and transfer to a plate.
6. Beat the eggs in a mixing bowl and stir in the cheeses.
7. Roll out the sausage and press it firmly into the bottom of a greased baking dish. Top with the chard mix.
8. Add the cheesy egg mixture over it. Cover the dish with foil.
9. Pour the water and place steamer basket/trivet inside the pot; arrange the baking dish over the basket/trivet.
10. Close the top lid and seal its valve.
11. Press "MANUAL" setting. Adjust cooking time to 25 minutes.
12. Allow the recipe to cook for the set cooking time.
13. After the set cooking time ends, press "CANCEL" and then press "NPR (Natural Pressure Release)".
14. Instant Pot will slowly and naturally release the pressure.
15. Open the top lid, add the cooked recipe mix in serving plates.
16. Serve and enjoy!

Nutritional Values (Per Serving):
Calories - 334
Fat – 27g
Carbohydrates – 12g
Fiber – 3.5g
Protein – 23g

Creamy Kale Eggs

Prep Time: 5 min.
Cooking Time: 5 min.
Number of Servings: 4

Ingredients:
- 3 tablespoons heavy cream
- 4 hard boiled eggs
- ¼ teaspoon pepper
- ¼ teaspoon salt
- 1 ½ cups water
- 4 kale leaves
- 4 prosciutto slices

Directions:
1. Peel the eggs and wrap them in kale. Wrap the eggs with prosciutto and sprinkle with pepper and salt.
2. Pour the water and place steamer basket/trivet inside the pot; arrange the eggs over the basket/trivet.
3. Press "MANUAL" setting. Adjust cooking time to 5 minutes.
4. Allow the recipe to cook for the set cooking time.
5. After the set cooking time ends, press "CANCEL" and then press "QPR (Quick Pressure Release)".
6. Instant Pot will quickly release the pressure.
7. Open the top lid.
8. Serve the eggs and enjoy!

Nutritional Values (Per Serving):

Calories - 243

Fat – 21.5g

Carbohydrates – 8g

Fiber – 2.5g

Protein – 15g

Spinach Avocado Breakfast Chicken

Prep Time: 5 min.
Cooking Time: 5 min.
Number of Servings: 3

Ingredients:
- 1 large leek, finely chopped
- 1 cup avocado chunks
- 1 small onion, finely chopped
- 7 ounce boneless and skinless chicken breast, make bite-sized pieces
- 1 cup fresh spinach, chopped
- 3 tablespoons butter
- 1 teaspoon salt
- 1 garlic clove, crushed
- 1 cup cottage cheese
- ½ teaspoon dried rosemary

Directions:
1. Take your Instant Pot; open the top lid. Plug it and turn it on.
2. Press "SAUTÉ" setting and the pot will start heating up.
3. In the cooking pot area, add the butter, salt, and meat. Stir and cook for 2-3 minutes until evenly brown from all sides.
4. Add the avocado and continue to cook for 2-3 minutes. If needed, add more butter.

5. Add the onions, garlic, and chopped leeks. Give it a good stir and cook to soften.
6. Add the spinach and sprinkle with rosemary.
7. Press "Cancel" button. Let it sit for 10 minutes and add the cooked recipe mix in serving plates.
8. Stir in the cottage cheese and serve immediately.

Nutritional Values (Per Serving):

Calories - 362

Fat – 24g

Carbohydrates – 9g

Fiber – 4g

Protein – 31g

Creamy Eggs & Turkey Bacon

Prep Time: 5 min.
Cooking Time: 5 min.
Number of Servings: 6

Ingredients:

- 1 cup cheddar cheese
- 1 cup kale leaves, chopped
- 6 eggs
- ½ cup heavy cream
- 1 cup turkey bacon (cooked)
- 1 cup water
- ⅛ tsp. sea salt
- 1 onion chopped
- ⅛ tsp. pepper
- 1 tsp. Herbes de Provence

Directions:

1. In a bowl, thoroughly mix the heavy cream and the eggs. Add leftover ingredients and combine well.
2. Add the mixture to a heatproof dish.
3. Arrange your Instant Pot over a dry, clean platform. Plug it in power socket and turn it on.
4. Slowly pour the water into the pot order to avoid spilling out. Take the trivet and arrange in the pot; place dish over the trivet.
5. Close the lid and lock. Ensure that you have sealed the valve to avoid leakage.

6. Press "Manual" mode from available cooking settings and set cooking time to 20 minutes. Instant Pot will start cooking the ingredients after a few minutes.
7. After the timer reads zero, press "Cancel" and quick release pressure.
8. Carefully remove the lid and serve the prepared keto dish warm!

Nutritional Values (Per Serving):

Calories – 284

Fat – 22g

Carbohydrates – 2.5g

Fiber – 1g

Protein – 16.5g

Chicken Herbal Breakfast

Prep Time: 5 min.

Cooking Time: 5 min.

Number of Servings: 5

Ingredients:

- 2 teaspoons basil
- ¼ cup heavy cream
- 13 ounce chicken fillet, strips
- 1 teaspoon salt
- 1 teaspoon cilantro
- 2 teaspoons oregano
- 1 teaspoon paprika
- 2 tablespoons melted butter

Directions:

1. In a bowl (medium or large size), thoroughly mix the salt, paprika, cilantro, oregano, and basil.
2. Top the chicken strips with the spices and cream; mix well.
3. Arrange your Instant Pot over a dry, clean platform. Plug it in power socket and turn it on.
4. Now press "Saute" mode from available options. In the cooking area, add the butter and strips; cook for 2-3 minutes to soften the added ingredients.
5. Close the lid and lock. Ensure that you have sealed the valve to avoid leakage.

6. Press "Manual" mode from available cooking settings and set cooking time to 20 minutes. Instant Pot will start cooking the ingredients after a few minutes.
7. After the timer reads zero, press "Cancel" and quick release pressure.
8. Carefully remove the lid and serve the prepared keto dish warm!

Nutritional Values (Per Serving):

Calories - 274

Fat – 21.8g

Carbohydrates – 1.5g

Fiber – 1g

Protein – 14g

Spinach Egg Breakfast Ramekins

Prep Time: 5 min.
Cooking Time: 5 min.
Number of Servings: 4

Ingredients:

- 1 cup chopped baby spinach
- 1 1/4 cup crumbled feta cheese
- 6 eggs
- ½ cup shredded mozzarella cheese
- 1 teaspoon pepper
- ¼ teaspoon garlic powder
- 1 tomato, chopped
- ½ teaspoon salt
- 1 ½ cups water

Directions:

1. In a mixing bowl, beat the eggs along with the spices. Stir in the tomato and cheeses.
2. Grease 4 ramekins and add the spinach. Pour the egg mixture over.
3. Pour the water and place steamer basket/trivet inside the pot; arrange the ramekins over the basket/trivet.
4. Close the top lid and seal its valve.
5. Press "MANUAL" setting. Adjust cooking time to 8 minutes.
6. Allow the recipe to cook for the set cooking time.

7. After the set cooking time ends, press "CANCEL" and then press "QPR (Quick Pressure Release)".
8. Instant Pot will quickly release the pressure.
9. Open the top lid, add the cooked recipe mix in serving plates.
10. Serve and enjoy!

Nutritional Values (Per Serving):
Calories - 116
Fat – 7.5g
Carbohydrates – 6g
Fiber – 3g
Protein – 11g

Chapter 5:

Chicken & Poultry Recipes

Broccoli Chicken Keto Treat

Prep Time: 5 min.
Cooking Time: 5 min.
Number of Servings: 4

Ingredients:
- 3 cups cooked and shredded chicken
- 2 cups broccoli florets
- 1/3 cup grated parmesan cheese
- ½ cup heavy cream
- 1 cup chicken broth
- Pepper and salt, as needed

Directions:
1. Take your Instant Pot; open the top lid. Plug it and turn it on.
2. In the cooking pot area, add the broth, broccoli, and chicken. Using a spatula, stir the ingredients.
3. Close the top lid and seal its valve.
4. Press "MANUAL" setting. Adjust cooking time to 2 minutes.
5. Allow the recipe to cook for the set cooking time.
6. After the set cooking time ends, press "CANCEL" and then press "QPR (Quick Pressure Release)".
7. Instant Pot will quickly release the pressure.
8. Open the top lid, stir in the remaining ingredients. Cook on sauté for 2 more minutes.
9. Serve and enjoy!

Nutritional Values (Per Serving):

Calories - 317

Fat – 23.5g

Carbohydrates – 6g

Fiber – 2g

Protein – 34g

Cheesy Turkey Bacon Chicken

Prep Time: 5 min.
Cooking Time: 5 min.
Number of Servings: 4

Ingredients:
- 8-ounces cream cheese
- 8 turkey bacon slices, cooked and crumbled
- 2 tablespoons arrowroot
- 1 cup water
- 2 pounds chicken breasts
- 1 packet ranch seasoning
- 4-ounces cheddar cheese, shredded

Directions:
1. Take your Instant Pot; open the top lid. Plug it and turn it on.
2. In the cooking pot area, add the cream cheese, water, chicken, and seasoning. Using a spatula, stir the ingredients.
3. Close the top lid and seal its valve.
4. Press "MANUAL" setting. Adjust cooking time to 25 minutes.
5. Allow the recipe to cook for the set cooking time.
6. After the set cooking time ends, press "CANCEL" and then press "QPR (Quick Pressure Release)".
7. Instant Pot will quickly release the pressure.
8. Open the top lid, take out the meat and shred it.

9. Add back to the mix and combine; add the remaining ingredients.
10. Cook on sauté for 3-4 minutes, add the cooked recipe mix in serving plates.
11. Serve and enjoy!

Nutritional Values (Per Serving):

Calories - 523

Fat – 38g

Carbohydrates – 8g

Fiber – 2.5g

Protein – 47.5g

Garlic Spiced Turkey

Prep Time: 5 min.
Cooking Time: 5 min.
Number of Servings: 2-3

Ingredients:
- 14-ounce turkey fillet, roughly chopped
- 1 teaspoon chili pepper
- 1 teaspoon (ground) black pepper
- 3 tablespoons chicken stock
- 1 garlic clove, chopped
- 1 teaspoon ghee
- 1 tomato, chopped
- 1 teaspoon olive oil
- 1 teaspoon cilantro
- ½ teaspoon chopped parsley

Directions:
1. Combine the chili pepper, (ground) black pepper, chopped tomato, olive oil, cilantro, chopped parsley, and chopped garlic clove in a mixing bowl.
2. Add the turkey fillet and chicken stock; stir it. Leave the mixture for 10 minutes to marinate.
3. Take your Instant Pot; open the top lid. Plug it and turn it on.
4. Press "SAUTÉ" setting, add the ghee and the pot will start heating up.

5. Add the chicken mix. Close the top lid and seal its valve.
6. Press "POULTRY" setting. Adjust cooking time to 15 minutes.
7. Allow the recipe to cook for the set cooking time.
8. After the set cooking time ends, press "CANCEL" and then press "QPR (Quick Pressure Release)".
9. Instant Pot will quickly release the pressure.
10. Open the top lid, add the cooked recipe mix in serving plates.
11. Serve and enjoy!

Nutritional Values (Per Serving):

Calories - 286

Fat – 12.5g

Carbohydrates – 2.5g

Fiber – 0.7g

Protein – 43.5g

Keto Chicken Drumsticks

Prep Time: 5 min.
Cooking Time: 5 min.
Number of Servings: 4

Ingredients:

- 1-pound chicken drumsticks
- 2 tablespoons coconut, shredded
- 2 tablespoons almond flour
- ½ teaspoon cayenne pepper
- 1 teaspoon olive oil
- 1 egg
- ¼ cup almond milk
- 1 teaspoon salt

Directions:

1. Combine the coconut and almond flour together in the mixing bowl. Mix in the almond milk and salt.
2. Add the cayenne pepper and olive oil. Stir the mixture.
3. Add the mixture into a large mixing bowl and add the chicken drumsticks.
4. Coat the chicken drumsticks in the coconut mixture.
5. Pour 1 cup water and place steamer basket/trivet inside the pot; arrange the drumsticks over the basket/trivet.
6. Close the top lid and seal its valve.

7. Press "POULTRY" setting. Adjust cooking time to 10 minutes.
8. Allow the recipe to cook for the set cooking time.
9. After the set cooking time ends, press "CANCEL" and then press "QPR (Quick Pressure Release)".
10. Instant Pot will quickly release the pressure.
11. Open the top lid, add the cooked recipe mix in serving plates.
12. Serve and enjoy!

Nutritional Values (Per Serving):

Calories - 246

Fat – 14.5g

Carbohydrates – 1g

Fiber – 0.3g

Protein – 31g

Lemon Mushroom Turkey

Prep Time: 5 min.
Cooking Time: 5 min.
Number of Servings: 8-10

Ingredients:
- 1 ¼ pounds turkey breast
- 1/3 cup lemon juice
- 6-ounces white button mushrooms, sliced
- 1 tablespoon arrowroot
- 2/3 cup chicken stock
- 3 tablespoons heavy cream
- 1 garlic clove, minced
- 3 tablespoon minced shallots
- 2 tablespoons olive oil
- ½ teaspoon parsley

Directions:
1. Take your Instant Pot; open the top lid. Plug it and turn it on.
2. Press "SAUTÉ" setting and the pot will start heating up.
3. In the cooking pot area, add the turkey and oil. Stir and cook until evenly brown from all sides. Set aside the cooked turkey.
4. Add the shallots, mushrooms, garlic, and parsley, and cook for a few more minutes.

5. Add back the turkey to the pot. Add the broth and stir gently.
6. Close the top lid and seal its valve.
7. Press "MANUAL" setting. Adjust cooking time to 8 minutes.
8. Allow the recipe to cook for the set cooking time.
9. After the set cooking time ends, press "CANCEL" and then press "QPR (Quick Pressure Release)".
10. Instant Pot will quickly release the pressure.
11. Open the top lid, slice the turkey and mix with the pot mix.
12. Mix in the cream and arrowroot; serve warm.

Nutritional Values (Per Serving):
Calories - 194
Fat – 16g
Carbohydrates – 7g
Fiber – 1.5g

Pumpkin Hot Chili

Prep Time: 8-10 min.
Cooking Time: 20 min.
Number of Servings: 5-6

Ingredients:

- 1 pound turkey, ground
- 1 (14.5 ounces) can diced tomatoes
- 1/2 cup Cheddar cheese, shredded
- 1/2 cup sour cream
- 2 cups pumpkin puree
- 1 1/2 tablespoons chili powder
- ¼ teaspoon oregano
- 1 tablespoon coconut oil
- 1 garlic clove, minced
- ¼ teaspoon cumin
- 1/2 teaspoon ground black pepper
- 1 dash salt
- 1 cup water

Directions:

1. Arrange your Instant Pot over a dry, clean platform. Plug it in power socket and turn it on.
2. Now press "Saute" mode from available options. In the cooking area, add the oil and turkey; cook to make it brown.
3. Add the garlic, onion, and pumpkin, mix well. Mix in the chili powder, salt, oregano, cumin; combine well.

4. Pour water into the pot.
5. Close the lid and lock. Ensure that you have sealed the valve to avoid leakage.
6. Press "Manual" mode from available cooking settings and set cooking time to 20 minutes. Instant Pot will start cooking the ingredients after a few minutes.
7. After the timer reads zero, press "Cancel" and quick release pressure.
8. Carefully remove the lid and serve the prepared keto dish warm topped with Cheddar cheese.

Nutritional Values (Per Serving):

Calories – 328

Fat – 20g

Carbohydrates – 8g

Fiber – 1g

Protein – 15.5g

Chapter 6:

Lamb And Beef Recipes

Keto Garlic Roast

Prep Time: 5 min.
Cooking Time: 5 min.
Number of Servings: 8-10

Ingredients:

- ½ cup onion, chopped
- 2 cups water
- ¼ teaspoon xanthan gum
- 1 teaspoon garlic powder
- 3-pound chuck roast, boneless
- ¼ cup balsamic vinegar
- Parsley, chopped to garnish
- 1 teaspoon pepper
- 1 tablespoon kosher salt

Directions:

1. Slice your roast in half and season with the garlic, pepper, and salt.
2. Arrange your Instant Pot over a dry, clean platform. Plug it in power socket and turn it on.
3. Now press "Saute" mode from available options. In the cooking area, add the meat; cook to brown.
4. Add the onion, water, and vinegar. Stir gently.
5. Close the lid and lock. Ensure that you have sealed the valve to avoid leakage.

6. Press "Manual" mode from available cooking settings and set cooking time to 35 minutes. Instant Pot will start cooking the ingredients after a few minutes.
7. After the timer reads zero, press "Cancel" and quick release pressure.
8. Carefully remove the lid. Carefully take the meat and make chunks.
9. Set the pot back on sauté; boil the mix for around 5 minutes.
10. Mix the gum and mix the shredded meat. Serve the prepared keto dish warm!

Nutritional Values (Per Serving):

Calories – 392

Fat – 28g

Carbohydrates – 3g

Fiber – 0g

Protein – 29.5g

Spicy Vinegar Lamb

Prep Time: 5 min.
Cooking Time: 5 min.
Number of Servings: 6

Ingredients:

- 1 tablespoon paprika
- 1 chili pepper, chopped
- 1 medium-size white onion, diced
- 1 tablespoon apple cider vinegar
- 1 pound lamb rack
- 1 teaspoon black pepper
- 1 teaspoon chili flakes
- 1 teaspoon olive oil

Directions:

1. Season the meat with the pepper and chili flakes. Sprinkle the lamb the vinegar and olive oil. Rub the meat with the paprika.
2. Arrange your Instant Pot over a dry, clean platform. Plug it in power socket and turn it on.
3. Open the lid from the top and put it aside; add the lamb, pepper, and onion.
4. Close the lid and lock. Ensure that you have sealed the valve to avoid leakage.
5. Press "Manual" mode from available cooking settings and set cooking time to 5 minutes. Instant Pot will start cooking the ingredients after a few minutes.

6. After the timer reads zero, press "Cancel" and quick release pressure.
7. Carefully remove the lid and serve the prepared keto dish warm!

Nutritional Values (Per Serving):
Calories - 148
Fat – 8.5g
Carbohydrates – 4g
Fiber – 1g
Protein – 15g

Sweet Potato Steak

Prep Time: 5 min.
Cooking Time: 5 min.
Number of Servings: 5

Ingredients:
- 2 teaspoons black pepper
- 1 tablespoon maple syrup
- 2 large sweet potatoes, peeled & cubed
- 1/2 cup beef broth
- 1 cup water
- 1/2 pound turkey bacon, sliced
- 2 tablespoons parsley
- 2 tablespoons thyme
- 1 tablespoon olive oil
- 5 carrots. make sticks
- 1 large red onion, sliced
- 1 pound flank steak
- 2 teaspoons rock salt
- 2 cloves garlic minced

Directions:
1. Pat dry the beef and season it.
2. Arrange your Instant Pot over a dry, clean platform. Plug it in power socket and turn it on.
3. Now press "Saute" mode from available options. In the cooking area, add the oil and beef; cook to brown evenly.

4. Add the onion, turkey bacon and other ingredients.
5. Close the lid and lock. Ensure that you have sealed the valve to avoid leakage.
6. Press "Manual" mode from available cooking settings and set cooking time to 5 minutes. Instant Pot will start cooking the ingredients after a few minutes.
7. After the timer reads zero, press "Cancel" and quick release pressure.
8. Carefully remove the lid and serve the prepared keto dish warm!

Nutritional Values (Per Serving):
Calories - 338
Fat – 19.5g
Carbohydrates – 17g
Fiber – 1.7g
Protein – 23.5g

Beef & Turkey Bacon Dinner Meal

Prep Time: 5 min.

Cooking Time: 5 min.

Number of Servings: 7-8

Ingredients:
- 3-ounce turkey bacon, sliced
- 2-pounds beef
- 9-ounce cabbage, chopped
- ½ cup water
- 2 garlic cloves, peeled, chopped

Directions:
1. Season the beef with the chopped garlic.
2. Take your Instant Pot; open the top lid. Plug it and turn it on.
3. In the cooking pot area, add the water and cabbage.
4. Top with the bacon and pork shoulder. Close the top lid and seal its valve.
5. Press "MANUAL" setting. Adjust cooking time to 5 minutes.
6. Allow the recipe to cook for the set cooking time.
7. After the set cooking time ends, press "CANCEL" and then press "NPR (Natural Pressure Release)".
8. Instant Pot will slowly and naturally release the pressure.
9. Open the top lid, add the cooked recipe mix in serving plates.
10. Serve and enjoy!

Nutritional Values (Per Serving):
Calories - 364
Fat – 28g
Carbohydrates – 2.5g
Fiber – 1g
Protein – 29g

Oregano Spiced Beef Chops

Prep Time: 5 min.
Cooking Time: 5 min.
Number of Servings: 2-3

Ingredients:
- 1 teaspoon dried dill
- 1-pound beef chops
- 1 teaspoon dried parsley
- ½ teaspoon coriander
- 1 teaspoon thyme
- 1 teaspoon oregano
- 1 tablespoon olive oil
- ¼ cup water
- ½ teaspoon salt

Directions:
1. Combine the thyme, oregano, dill, parsley, coriander, salt, and olive oil in a mixing bowl. Stir the mixture and mix the chops with the spice mix.
2. Close the top lid and seal its valve.
3. Press "MANUAL" setting. Adjust cooking time to 25 minutes.
4. Allow the recipe to cook for the set cooking time.
5. After the set cooking time ends, press "CANCEL" and then press "NPR (Natural Pressure Release)".
6. Instant Pot will slowly and naturally release the pressure.

7. Open the top lid, add the cooked recipe mix in serving plates.
8. Serve and enjoy!

Nutritional Values (Per Serving):
Calories - 326
Fat – 17.5g
Carbohydrates – 5.5g
Fiber – 0.5g
Protein – 46g

Milky Beef Roast

Prep Time: 5 min.
Cooking Time: 5 min.
Number of Servings: 7-8

Ingredients:
- 1 tablespoon paprika
- 2-pounds beef roast
- 1 cup almond milk
- 1 teaspoon salt
- 1 teaspoon raw honey

Directions:
1. Combine the almond milk and salt in a mixing bowl. Add the paprika and raw honey. Stir the mixture well; add the beef roast in the almond milk mixture and leave for 5 minutes.
2. Take your Instant Pot; open the top lid. Plug it and turn it on.
3. In the cooking pot area, add the bowl mix. Using a spatula, stir the ingredients.
4. Close the top lid and seal its valve.
5. Press "MANUAL" setting. Adjust cooking time to 30 minutes.
6. Allow the recipe to cook for the set cooking time.
7. After the set cooking time ends, press "CANCEL" and then press "QPR (Quick Pressure Release)".
8. Instant Pot will quickly release the pressure.

9. Open the top lid, add the cooked recipe mix in serving plates.
10. Serve and enjoy!

Nutritional Values (Per Serving):
Calories - 284
Fat – 14.5g
Carbohydrates – 3g
Fiber – 1g
Protein – 34g

Chapter 7:

Seafood Recipes

Cheddar Creamy Haddock

Prep Time: 5 min.
Cooking Time: 5 min.
Number of Servings: 4

Ingredients:

-
- ½ cup heavy cream
- 5-ounces cheddar cheese, grated
- 3 tablespoons diced onions
- 12-ounces haddock fillets
- 1 tablespoon butter
- ¼ teaspoon garlic salt
- ¼ teaspoon pepper

Directions:

1. Take your Instant Pot; open the top lid. Plug it and turn it on.
2. Press "SAUTÉ" setting and the pot will start heating up.
3. In the cooking pot area, add the butter and onions. Cook until starts becoming translucent and softened for 3 minutes. Stir in between.
4. Season the fish with pepper and salt. Add the fish in the pot and cook for 2 minutes per side. Pour the cream over and top with the cheese.
5. Close the top lid and seal its valve.
6. Press "MANUAL" setting. Adjust cooking time to 5 minutes.

7. Allow the recipe to cook for the set cooking time.
8. After the set cooking time ends, press "CANCEL" and then press "NPR (Natural Pressure Release)".
9. Instant Pot will slowly and naturally release the pressure.
10. Open the top lid, add the cooked recipe mix in serving plates.
11. Serve and enjoy!

Nutritional Values (Per Serving):

Calories – 192

Fat – 17.5g

Carbohydrates – 5g

Fiber – 1g

Protein – 18g

Tangy Orange Trout

Prep Time: 5 min.
Cooking Time: 5 min.
Number of Servings: 4

Ingredients:
- 2-ounce lemon, juiced
- 1 teaspoon lemon zest
- ¼ orange, juiced
- 1 tablespoon smoked paprika
- 14-ounce trout
- 1 teaspoon sea salt
- ½ teaspoon oregano
- 1 teaspoon honey
- 1 tablespoon olive oil

Directions:
1. Chop the trout into 4 medium pieces.
2. Mix the lemon, orange, sea salt, oregano, honey, and olive oil in a mixing bowl.
3. Coat the trout with the lemon mixture from each side.
4. Take your Instant Pot; open the top lid. Plug it and turn it on.
5. Pour the water and place steamer basket/trivet inside the pot; arrange the trout over the basket/trivet.
6. Close the top lid and seal its valve.
7. Press "STEAM" setting. Adjust cooking time to 5 minutes.

8. Allow the recipe to cook for the set cooking time.
9. After the set cooking time ends, press "CANCEL" and then press "QPR (Quick Pressure Release)".
10. Instant Pot will quickly release the pressure.
11. Open the top lid, add the cooked recipe mix in serving plates.
12. Serve and enjoy!

Nutritional Values (Per Serving):

Calories - 238

Fat – 13g

Carbohydrates – 5g

Fiber – 1.5g

Protein – 27g

Shrimp Zoodles Meal

Prep Time: 5 min.
Cooking Time: 5 min.
Number of Servings: 4

Ingredients:

- 1 cup veggie stock
- 2 tablespoons olive oil
- 3 teaspoons minced garlic
- 4 cups zucchini noodles
- 2 tablespoon ghee
- Juice of ½ lemon
- 1 tablespoon chopped basil
- 1-pound shrimp, peeled and deveined
- ½ teaspoon paprika

Directions:

1. Take your Instant Pot; open the top lid. Plug it and turn it on.
2. Press "SAUTÉ" setting and the pot will start heating up.
3. In the cooking pot area, add the oil, ghee, and garlic.
4. Cook for 1 minute and add the shrimp and lemon juice.
5. Cook for 1 more minute. Add the zoodles, paprika, and stock.
6. Close the top lid and seal its valve.

7. Press "MANUAL" setting. Adjust cooking time to 3 minutes.
8. Allow the recipe to cook for the set cooking time.
9. After the set cooking time ends, press "CANCEL" and then press "QPR (Quick Pressure Release)".
10. Instant Pot will quickly release the pressure.
11. Open the top lid, add the cooked recipe mix in serving plates. Top with basil.
12. Serve and enjoy!

Nutritional Values (Per Serving):
Calories - 287
Fat – 19.5g
Carbohydrates – 5g
Fiber – 3g
Protein – 29g

Shrimp Sausage Meal

Prep Time: 5 min.
Cooking Time: 5 min.
Number of Servings: 4

Ingredients:
- 1 tablespoon old bay
- 4 ears of corn, chopped
- 2 yellow onions, chopped
- 1 teaspoon red pepper flakes, crushed
- 16 ounces beer
- 12 ounces sliced and cooked chicken sausage
- 1½ pounds deveined shrimp
- Black pepper and salt as needed
- 8 minced garlic cloves

Directions:
1. Arrange your Instant Pot over a dry, clean platform. Plug it in power socket and turn it on.
2. Open the lid from the top and put it aside; add the ingredients and gently stir them.
3. Close the lid and lock. Ensure that you have sealed the valve to avoid leakage.
4. Press "Manual" mode from available cooking settings and set cooking time to 5 minutes. Instant Pot will start cooking the ingredients after a few minutes.
5. After the timer reads zero, press "Cancel" and quick release pressure.

6. Carefully remove the lid and serve the prepared keto dish warm!

Nutritional Values (Per Serving):
Calories – 208
Fat – 25g
Carbohydrates – 8g
Fiber – 1.5g
Protein – 16.5g

Herbed Trout Fillet

Prep Time: 5 min.
Cooking Time: 5 min.
Number of Servings: 4

Ingredients:
- 1 teaspoon stevia
- 1/2 cup basil, chopped
- 1 teaspoon black pepper
- 1 teaspoon dried dill
- 1 pound trout fillet, divide into pieces
- 1 teaspoon fresh ginger, crushed

Directions:
1. Season the fish with the pepper and dill. Add the sugar and stir gently.
2. Top with the basil and ginger; set aside for 8-10 minutes.
3. Arrange your Instant Pot over a dry, clean platform. Plug it in power socket and turn it on.
4. Open the lid from the top and put it aside; add the fish and marinade. Gently stir them.
5. Close the lid and lock. Ensure that you have sealed the valve to avoid leakage.
6. Press "Manual" mode from available cooking settings and set cooking time to 15 minutes. Instant Pot will start cooking the ingredients after a few minutes.

7. After the timer reads zero, press "Cancel" and quick release pressure.
8. Carefully remove the lid and serve the prepared keto dish warm!

Nutritional Values (Per Serving):

Calories - 175

Fat – 7.5g

Carbohydrates – 1.5g

Fiber – 0g

Protein – 19.5g

Garlic Shrimp with Rice

Prep Time: 5 min.
Cooking Time: 5 min.
Number of Servings: 4-5

Ingredients:

- 1½ cup water
- Juice of 1 lemon
- Crushed red pepper
- ¼ cup chopped parsley
- Black pepper and sea salt as needed
- 1 cup jasmine rice
- 20 large deveined shrimp
- ¼ cup ghee
- A pinch of saffron
- 4 minced garlic cloves
- Grated cheddar cheese as needed

Directions:

1. Arrange your Instant Pot over a dry, clean platform. Plug it in power socket and turn it on.
2. Now press "Saute" mode from available options. In the cooking area, add some water and rice; cook for 1 minutes.
3. Add the shrimps, ghee, parsley, salt, pepper, red pepper, lemon juice, saffron, garlic, and water. Stir well.

4. Close the lid and lock. Ensure that you have sealed the valve to avoid leakage.
5. Press "Manual" mode from available cooking settings and set cooking time to 5 minutes. Instant Pot will start cooking the ingredients after a few minutes.
6. After the timer reads zero, press "Cancel" and quick release pressure.
7. Carefully remove the lid. Peel the shrimps and divide them between on plates.
8. Add the parsley, cheese and rice mix on top. Serve the prepared keto dish warm!

Nutritional Values (Per Serving):

Calories – 252

Fat – 34.5g

Carbohydrates – 7g

Fiber – 0.3g

Protein – 20g

Raspberry Salmon

Prep Time: 5 min.
Cooking Time: 5 min.
Number of Servings: 5-6

Ingredients:

- 2 garlic cloves, minced
- 1 cup clam juice
- 2 tablespoons parsley, chopped
- 2 tablespoons lemon juice
- 4 leeks, chopped
- 2 tablespoons olive oil
- 6 salmon steaks
- Sea salt black pepper and salt as needed
- 2 pints red raspberries
- 1/3 cup dill, chopped
- 1 teaspoon sherry
- 1-pint cider vinegar

Directions:

1. Mix the berries and vinegar in a bowl and stir well. Mix in the salmon, stir, cover and keep in the fridge for 2 hours.
2. Arrange your Instant Pot over a dry, clean platform. Plug it in power socket and turn it on.
3. Now press "Saute" mode from available options. In the cooking area, add the garlic, parsley, and leeks; cook for 2-3 minutes to soften.

4. Add the lemon juice, clam juice, salt, pepper, cherry, and dill; stir well and cook for 2 minutes. Add the salmon and stir well.
5. Close the lid and lock. Ensure that you have sealed the valve to avoid leakage.
6. Press "Manual" mode from available cooking settings and set cooking time to 4 minutes. Instant Pot will start cooking the ingredients after a few minutes.
7. After the timer reads zero, press "Cancel"; press "NPR" to naturally release pressure. It takes about 8-10 minutes to release pressure naturally.
8. Carefully remove the lid and serve the prepared keto dish warm!

Nutritional Values (Per Serving):
Calories – 158
Fat – 25g
Carbohydrates – 5.5g
Fiber – 1g
Protein – 12g

Chapter 9:

Keto Snacks

Cashew Hummus

Prep Time: 5 min.
Cooking Time: 1 min.
Number of Servings: 5-6

Ingredients:
- 1 lemon, juiced
- 4 cloves garlic
- ½ teaspoon sea salt
- 1 teaspoon red pepper flakes
- 1 1/2 cups cashews
- ½ teaspoon cumin
- 2 tablespoons tahini
- ½ cup extra-virgin olive oil
- Handful of parsley

Directions:
1. Take your Instant Pot; open the top lid. Plug it and turn it on.
2. Press "SAUTÉ" setting and the pot will start heating up.
3. In the cooking pot area, add the oil and garlic. Cook for only 10 seconds.
4. Take a blender and add the cooked garlic and remaining ingredients.
5. Blend well and serve the hummus with vegetable sticks or low carb crackers.

Nutritional Values (Per Serving):

Calories - 474

Fat – 41g

Carbohydrates – 11g

Fiber – 2g

Protein – 7g

Seasoned Peanut Mania

Prep Time: 5 min.
Cooking Time: 5 min.
Number of Servings: 5-6

Ingredients:

- ¼ cup kosher salt
- ¼ cup apple cider vinegar
- 1 pound raw peanuts with shells
- 1/3 cup Old Bay seasoning
- 1 tablespoon mustard seeds
- 1 bay leaf
- Water, as required

Directions:

1. Take your Instant Pot; open the top lid. Plug it and turn it on.
2. In the cooking pot area, add all the ingredients and enough water to cover all ingredients.
3. Close the top lid and seal its valve.
4. Press "MANUAL" setting. Adjust cooking time to 5 minutes.
5. Allow the recipe to cook for the set cooking time.
6. After the set cooking time ends, press "CANCEL" and then press "NPR (Natural Pressure Release)".
7. Instant Pot will slowly and naturally release the pressure.

8. Open the top lid, add the cooked recipe mix in serving plates.
9. Drain liquid and serve.

Nutritional Values (Per Serving):
Calories - 532
Fat – 37g
Carbohydrates – 11g
Fiber – 7g
Protein – 20g

Cheddar Chicken Dip

Prep Time: 5 min.
Cooking Time: 5 min.
Number of Servings: 7-8

Ingredients:
- 16 ounces cheddar cheese
- 1 stick butter
- 1 packet ranch dip mix
- 1 cup cream cheese
- 1 pound chicken breast
- 1 cup hot sauce

Directions:
1. Arrange your Instant Pot over a dry, clean platform. Plug it in power socket and turn it on.
2. Open the lid from the top and put it aside; add the ranch, sauce, butter, cream cheese, and chicken and gently stir them.
3. Close the lid and lock. Ensure that you have sealed the valve to avoid leakage.
4. Press "Manual" mode from available cooking settings and set cooking time to 15 minutes. Instant Pot will start cooking the ingredients after a few minutes.
5. After the timer reads zero, press "Cancel" and quick release pressure.
6. Carefully remove the lid and shred up the chicken with a fork.

7. Mix the cheddar cheese and serve with low carb chips or veggies.

Nutritional Values (Per Serving):
Calories – 389
Fat – 40.5g
Carbohydrates – 2.5g
Fiber – 0.2g
Protein – 29g

Keto Zucchini Bites

Prep Time: 5 min.
Cooking Time: 2-3 min.
Number of Servings: 6

Ingredients:
- 1/2 teaspoon white pepper
- 1 cup coconut
- 3 tablespoons butter
- 1 teaspoon salt
- 4 tablespoons almond flour
- 1 medium size egg
- 1 zucchini, grated

Directions:
1. In a bowl (medium or large size), whisk the eggs. Add the almond flour, coconut, salt, and pepper.
2. Add the zucchini and mix well. Make small balls.
3. Arrange your Instant Pot over a dry, clean platform. Plug it in power socket and turn it on.
4. Coat the inner surface with the butter.
5. Now press "Saute" mode from available options. In the cooking area, add the balls; cook for a few minutes to brown the balls.
6. Enjoy them warm!

Nutritional Values (Per Serving):
Calories - 91

Fat – 8g

Carbohydrates – 2.5g

Fiber – 1g

Protein – 3.5g

Almond Zucchini Balls

Prep Time: 5 min.
Cooking Time: 4 min.
Number of Servings: 56

Ingredients:
- 1/2 teaspoon white pepper
- 1 cup coconut
- 4 tablespoons almond flour
- 3 tablespoons butter
- 1 teaspoon salt
- 1 egg
- 1 zucchini, grated

Directions:
1. In a bowl, whisk the eggs. Add the almond flour, coconut, salt, and white pepper.
2. Add the zucchini and combine; make small balls from the mix.
3. Take your Instant Pot; open the top lid. Plug it and turn it on.
4. Press "SAUTÉ" setting and the pot will start heating up.
5. In the cooking pot area, add the butter and balls.
6. Heat to brown the balls. Serve warm!

Nutritional Values (Per Serving):
Calories - 91

Fat – 8g
Carbohydrates – 2.5g
Fiber – 1g
Protein – 3g

Chapter 10:

Desserts

Avocado Choco Treat

Prep Time: 5 min.
Cooking Time: 5 min.
Number of Servings: 5

Ingredients:
- 1/4 teaspoon cinnamon
- 1 avocado, chopped and pitted
- 1 cup heavy cream
- 2 teaspoons sugar
- 1 medium size egg
- 1 ounce dark chocolate
- 1/4 tablespoon chia seeds

Directions:
1. Add the cream, sugar, and avocado in a blender. Blend to make a smooth mixture.
2. Beat the egg in a bowl and add it in the blender. Add the ground cinnamon and combine.
3. Ads the chocolate and blend the mixture.
4. Arrange your Instant Pot over a dry, clean platform. Plug it in power socket and turn it on.
5. Open the lid from the top and put it aside; add the mixture and top with the chia seeds.
6. Close the lid and lock. Ensure that you have sealed the valve to avoid leakage.

7. Press "Manual" mode from available cooking settings and set cooking time to 10 minutes. Instant Pot will start cooking the ingredients after a few minutes.
8. After the timer reads zero, press "Cancel" and quick release pressure.
9. Carefully remove the lid and serve the prepared keto dish warm!

Nutritional Values (Per Serving):

Calories - 258

Fat – 23.5g

Carbohydrates – 9g

Fiber – 3.5g

Protein – 5g

Choco Almond Pudding

Prep Time: 5 min.
Cooking Time: 5 min.
Number of Servings: 4

Ingredients:
- 1 tablespoon agar powder
- ¼ cup almonds, finely chopped
- 2 tablespoons cocoa powder, unsweetened
- 1 cup unsweetened almond milk
- ¼ cup swerve
- 2 tablespoon chocolate chips, sugar-free
- 1 ¼ cup whipping cream
- ½ cup coconut cream
- 1 teaspoon vanilla extract

Directions:
1. Take your Instant Pot; open the top lid. Plug it and turn it on.
2. Press "SAUTÉ" setting and the pot will start heating up.
3. Pour in the milk, swerve, cocoa powder, coconut cream, and vanilla extract.
4. Bring it to a boil, stirring constantly, and then add the agar powder.
5. Continue to cook for 1-2 minutes.
6. Press ''Cancel'' button and mix the almonds.

7. Transfer the mix to a blender and pour in the whipping cream. Beat well on high speed for 2-3 minutes.
8. Add the mixture between serving bowls and chill in the refrigerator. Serve chilled.

Nutritional Values (Per Serving):

Calories - 248

Fat – 24g

Carbohydrates – 9g

Fiber – 3g

Protein – 3.5g

Cherry Pecan Mousse

Prep Time: 5 min.
Cooking Time: 5 min.
Number of Servings: 5-6

Ingredients:
- 1 tablespoon pecans, minced
- ¼ cup erythritol
- 1 ½ cup whipping cream
- 5 large egg yolks, beaten
- ½ cup whole milk
- ½ cup coconut cream
- ½ teaspoon salt
- 2 teaspoon cherry extract

Directions:
1. Take your Instant Pot; open the top lid. Plug it and turn it on.
2. Press "SAUTÉ" setting and the pot will start heating up.
3. Add the whipping cream, egg yolks, erythritol, milk, salt, and coconut cream; boil the mix.
4. Cool down the mix and pour the mixture into heat-safe ramekins.
5. Sprinkle with pecans and wrap each ramekin with aluminum foil.
6. Take your Instant Pot; open the top lid. Plug it and turn it on.

7. Pour 1 cup water and place steamer basket/trivet inside the pot; arrange the ramekins over the basket/trivet.
8. Close the top lid and seal its valve.
9. Press "MANUAL" setting. Adjust cooking time to 7 minutes.
10. Allow the recipe to cook for the set cooking time.
11. After the set cooking time ends, press "CANCEL" and then press "QPR (Quick Pressure Release)".
12. Instant Pot will quickly release the pressure.
13. Open the top lid, cool down the ramekins.
14. Refrigerate for at least an hour before serving.

Nutritional Values (Per Serving):

Calories - 223

Fat – 21g

Carbohydrates – 13g

Fiber – 1.5g

Protein – 4g

Creamy Strawberry Pudding

Prep Time: 5 min.
Cooking Time: 5 min.
Number of Servings: 4-5

Ingredients:
- 2 cups heavy cream
- 1 tablespoon butter
- 1/4 cup strawberries, mashed
- 1 tablespoon Erythritol
- 1 teaspoon chia seeds
- 1 tablespoon tapioca

Directions:
1. Arrange your Instant Pot over a dry, clean platform. Plug it in power socket and turn it on.
2. Now press "Saute" mode from available options. In the cooking area, add the cream; cook for 4-5 minutes to soften.
3. Add the tapioca and stir it well. Mix the Erythritol and butter.
4. In a bowl (medium or large size), mix the chia seeds and berries. Add the berry mixture to the pot and stir it gently.
5. Close the lid and lock. Ensure that you have sealed the valve to avoid leakage.

6. Press "Saute" mode from available cooking settings and set cooking time to 15 minutes. Instant Pot will start cooking the ingredients after a few minutes.
7. After the timer reads zero, press "Cancel" and quick release pressure.
8. Carefully remove the lid. Refrigerate and serve chilled!

Nutritional Values (Per Serving):

Calories - 281

Fat – 26g

Carbohydrates – 9.5g

Fiber – 2g

Protein – 2.3g

Chocolate Cake

Prep Time: 5 min.
Cooking Time: 5 min.
Number of Servings: 5

Ingredients:
- ⅔ cup Erythritol
- 4 tablespoons cocoa powder, unsweetened
- ½ cup almond flour
- ¼ teaspoon vanilla extract
- 2 medium size eggs
- 4 tablespoons butter
- 2 tablespoons chocolate chips

Directions:
1. Melt the chips and butter in a microwave in a bowl (heat-safe) for 1 minute.
2. Add the Erythritol and whisk to combine. Add the vanilla and egg, and mix again.
3. Add the cocoa and flour; mix until blended. Add the mixture to ramekins; spread it gently.
4. Arrange your Instant Pot over a dry, clean platform. Plug it in power socket and turn it on.
5. Slowly pour the water into the pot order to avoid spilling out. Take the trivet and arrange in the pot; place the ramekins over the trivet.
6. Close the lid and lock. Ensure that you have sealed the valve to avoid leakage.

7. Press "Manual" mode from available cooking settings and set cooking time to 18 minutes. Instant Pot will start cooking the ingredients after a few minutes.
8. After the timer reads zero, press "Cancel" and quick release pressure.
9. Carefully remove the lid. Make squares and serve warm!

Nutritional Values (Per Serving):
Calories – 184
Fat – 16g
Carbohydrates – 10g
Fiber – 4g
Protein – 5.5g

Vanilla Orange Muffins

Prep Time: 5 min.
Cooking Time: 5 min.
Number of Servings: 8

Ingredients:
- 1/2 teaspoon baking powder
- 1 tablespoon orange juice
- 1/4 cup cream cheese
- 5 tablespoons butter
- 3 tablespoons almond flour
- 4 tablespoons granular stevia or sugar
- 1 teaspoon vanilla extract
- 1 cup coconut flour

Directions:
1. Mix the butter and cheese in a blender. Mix in the baking powder and juice.
2. Mix in both the flours. Top the mixture of the stevia/sugar and vanilla extract.
3. Blend for 1 more minute to prepare a thick dough-like mixture. Pour into the lightly greased muffin tins.
4. Open the lid from the top and put it aside; add the tins and gently stir them.
5. Close the lid and lock. Ensure that you have sealed the valve to avoid leakage.

6. Press "Manual" mode from available cooking settings and set cooking time to 10 minutes. Instant Pot will start cooking the ingredients after a few minutes.
7. After the timer reads zero, press "Cancel" and quick release pressure.
8. Carefully remove the lid and serve the prepared keto dish warm!

Nutritional Values (Per Serving):

Calories - 93

Fat – 9.5g

Carbohydrates – 2g

Fiber – 0.4g

Protein – 1.5g

Orange Choco Muffins

Prep Time: 5 min.
Cooking Time: 5 min.
Number of Servings: 4-5

Ingredients:
- 1 tablespoon chia seeds
- 1 tablespoon flaxseed meal
- ½ cup whole milk
- ½ cup almond flour
- ¼ cup almonds, roughly chopped
- 5 large eggs
- 1 tablespoon butter
- ¼ teaspoon bicarbonate of soda
- 1 tablespoon dark chocolate chips
- ½ teaspoon baking powder
- 1 teaspoon orange extract
- 2 teaspoons stevia powder
- ¼ teaspoon cinnamon, ground

Directions:
1. In a mixing bowl, combine the flour, almonds, chia seeds, flaxseed meal, baking powder, and bicarbonate soda.
2. Mix until well combined. Add the eggs, butter, milk, orange extract, stevia, and cinnamon.
3. Add the mix in a blender and make a smooth mix.

4. Divide into greased muffin molds. Top with the chocolate chips and set aside.
5. Take your Instant Pot; open the top lid. Plug it and turn it on.
6. Pour the water and place steamer basket/trivet inside the pot; arrange the molds over the basket/trivet.
7. Close the top lid and seal its valve.
8. Press "MANUAL" setting. Adjust cooking time to 30 minutes.
9. Allow the recipe to cook for the set cooking time.
10. After the set cooking time ends, press "CANCEL" and then press "QPR (Quick Pressure Release)".
11. Instant Pot will quickly release the pressure.
12. Open the top lid, cool down the molds.
13. Serve and enjoy!

Nutritional Values (Per Serving):
Calories – 232
Fat – 18.5g
Carbohydrates – 9g
Fiber – 4g
Protein – 11g

Maintaining the Results of the Diet

Sustainability is the biggest problem with all diets.

You CAN get results with keto.

You CAN get results with Atkins.

You CAN get results being a vegan.

You CAN get results with If It Fits Your Macros.

You CAN get results with the Mediterranean diet.

But if you're just looking for a short term change, you'll only get short term results.

You'll gain weight again.

Bummer.

When you are in Week 4 of the Keto diet, you need to think of more permanent solutions to allow your body to naturally burn fat and stay fit for longer. This doesn't mean that you cannot consume carbohydrates again, but it means that you need to know how to use food and exercise to your advantage.

There's a reason #ketolife is such a popular hashtag.

It's not meant to be a diet, it's meant to be a lifestyle.

Keto, Quick and Easy (just like we promised!)

Keto started nearly a century ago under medical supervision for totally different reasons and this is why you need to expect some other health benefits in the area of cognition as well.

A few quick tips:

- **Use Our Recipes**: Use our 5-minute recipes to make quick and easy meals that hit the spot
- **The "Keto Flu"**: Your first days on the diet will also be the hardest. The best way to tackle it is to start consuming fats to have an energy source in your body which allows you to minimize this potential issue.
- **Track What You Eat**: It's a good idea to look at the foods which, at the end of the day, need to be around the 75% fats, 20% protein and 5% carbs ratio. The closer you are to this, the better. If you are unsure, you always need to increase fat consumption as it is largely responsible for satiety and it will keep you on track with controlling cravings as well.

The Keto diet is also largely different to what it was in the early 1900s. You do not have to wait weeks to see if you lose weight or even if you are in the state of ketosis. You can use one of the outlined testing methods to establish your ketone levels on the spot.

Leave a Review

Please leave a review. It'll mean a LOT to us.

Plus, it's quick and easy (see what we did there?)

Printed in Great Britain
by Amazon